2

ARROWS
OF THE
ALMIGHTY

*The Story of William Bromley,
Pioneer Missionary
to Papua New Guinea*

A. A. E. BERG

ISBN-083-411-531X

W0008741

Nazarene Publishing House
Kansas City, Missouri

First Printing 1972
Second Edition (abridged) Copyright 1995
by Nazarene Publishing House

ISBN 083-411-531X

Printed in the
United States of America

Cover Design: Crandal Vail and Michael Walsh
Illustration: Keith Alexander

All Scripture quotations are from the King James Version of the Bible.

10   9   8   7   6   5   4   3   2   1

May the selflessness and Christian fragrance
that characterized the life of Missionary
William Ewart Bromley
be reflected in his young son, John William,
to whom this book is affectionately dedicated.

RESOURCE BOOK FOR THE LEADER

TOUCHING LIVES THROUGH SHARING
Edited by Beverlee Borbe

FOR THE READER

ARROWS OF THE ALMIGHTY
The Story of William Bromley,
Pioneer Missionary to Papua New Guinea
By A. A. E. Berg

FURLOUGHS, FURLONGS, AND POTLUCK DINNERS
Stories from the Deputation Trail
By A. Brent Cobb

MY LIFE AMONG THE NAVAJO
A Ministry to Body and Soul
By Beulah Campbell

RUN WITH THE TORCH
The Church of the Nazarene in El Salvador
By Eunice Bryant

BRINGING GOD'S WORD TO GUATEMALA
The Life and Work of William and Betty Sedat
By Lorraine O. Schultz

TREASURES IN THE DARKNESS
Stories from Behind Broken Walls
By Sharon R. Martin

CONTENTS

Preface   7

Acknowledgments   9

1. Called—Chosen—Faithful   11

2. God's Guiding Hand   16

3. The Wahgi   24

4. The Jimi   31

5. Laying Foundations   40

6. Visiting Tsingoropa   47

7. "It's Coming, Dear Brother;
   I Know It's Coming"   56

8. "All Right, Lord, It's Over to You"   63

9. The Homegoing   70

10. Love's Legacy   76

Epilogue—"The Rest of the Story"   84
   (Robert H. Scott)

Reverend Doctor A. A. E. Berg joined the Church of the Nazarene in May 1945 in order to begin the work of the church in Australia. He subsequently served as district superintendent of the Australian District from 1948 until his death in 1979. Rev. Berg had a long-standing burden for the people of the Territories of Papua New Guinea (now Papua New Guinea) making the first official visit for the Church of the Nazarene in 1954. He made several subsequent visits in later years as the work in New Guinea was established.

PREFACE

Will Bromley was a quiet man, short of stature, slow of speech, and slow in his movements. He was almost always smiling and had an air of casualness about him that made it difficult for most people to assess his true qualities. Not a few of his friends were tempted to wonder how this genial, gentle-mannered Christian missionary could effectively break through a raw heathen culture with the message of the gospel. On the surface, he appeared to be inadequately equipped for the task of working alone among the many thousands of Jimi Valley tribespeople who had been, until recently, involved in bitter intertribal wars and revenge killings and whose animistic way of life was in such direct contrast to his own.

However, those who were intimately acquainted with Will knew him to be a man of courage and strong conviction. When truth or principle was at stake, he was bold as a lion; when under stress, he was calm and confident in God. His spiritual strength was due to a close walk with God and being found often at the place of prayer. He had learned to prevail with God while on his knees.

When a servant of the Lord has finished his work and his life's race has been run, there is a vantage point of perspective from which one can detect the guiding hand of God from childhood to the grave. As we live our lives we cannot see the future, and thus it must be if we are to continue in faith. But we are persuaded that, for all who have committed their lives unto the Heavenly Father's care and direction, there will be a final chapter written that will more than justify the disappointments, testings, and apparent calamities of the yesteryears.

Will Bromley was a pliable instrument in the skillfull hands of God, and God used this instrument, guided by His all-seeing eye, to direct His arrows of conviction to many a sin-sodden, heathen heart. The "arrows of the Almighty" never fail to strike their target through the medium of a yielded, Christ-centered life. As New Guinea bowmen know, it takes a supple bow, a taut string, and the direction of a keen eye for the arrow to find its mark.

Editor's Note—The territory that in this book is called New Guinea is the northern part of the nation of Papua New Guinea. Words from Papua New Guinea can be pronounced as they appear if the following guidelines are observed:

a is always ah as in father

o is almost always short

i is short except at the end of a word, where it is pronounced ee.

ACKNOWLEDGMENTS

My sincere thanks go to several wonderful friends who have willingly supplied much-needed information for this story. Mrs. Margaret Bromley, Mr. Clem Bromley, and Rev. Wallace F. White have been specially helpful. Thanks are also due to Mrs. Joyce Bartle and Mr. Jim Grimes for the use of tape recordings, and to my daughter, Marion Isobel, for typing the manuscript. Above all, I want to thank God for His enablements, without which this biography could not have been written.

—A. A. E. BERG

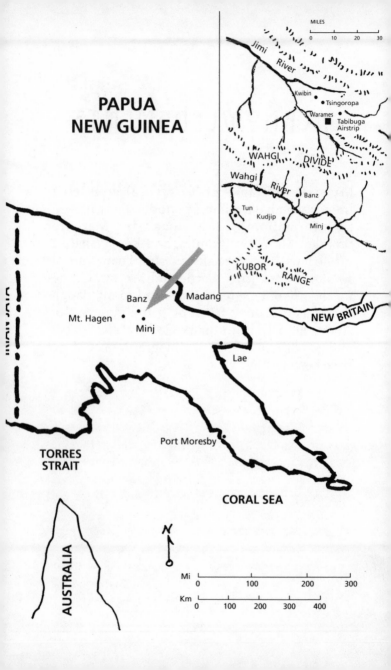

Called—Chosen—Faithful

WILLIAM EWART BROMLEY was born in the city of Worcester in Worcestershire, England, on August 15, 1905. He was the second of four children. His parents, Frederick and Helen Bromley, with Eustace, William, Clement, and Elizabeth, later moved to the town of Nineveh in Staffordshire, where they made their family home.

Frederick was a Methodist local preacher, and Helen, a member of the Church of England. They were both true Christians and united in their efforts to rear their four children in the ways of the Lord. Helen frequently recounted to them in simple terms the New Testament stories of Jesus and taught them to pray and memorize Scripture. These early influences upon the children were never lost. However, their happy and wholesome life with Mother was short-lived, for she passed away suddenly when Will was eight years old.

Fred carried on as best he could, trusting God for grace and strength in his deep sorrow. He loved to preach the gospel and faithfully con-

tinued his services in the local Methodist circuit.
On not a few occasions, while Fred was in the
pulpit, young Will would quietly move out of his
pew and take his place beside his father. He
would then hold him by the hand and stand rev-
erently at his side until the close of his sermon. It
appeared that Will, even at that early age, wanted to be identified with his dad as he proclaimed
the gospel.

Fred had come to realize, rather ruefully,
that he could not provide for his children as their
many needs demanded. After much prayer, he
decided to go to London to pursue his profession
as an interior decorator and see if he could make
a better life for his family. It was arranged for
William and Clement to live with an aunt, Miss
Millie Bell, who lived at Pershore in Staffordshire. She gladly took the boys into her loving
care and brought them with her to the Church of
England where she was a member.

A monk, who was engaged in the service of
this church in Pershore, and who lived in the
nearby abbey, began to take a keen interest in the
spiritual welfare of the two boys who had recently lost their mother. He was a man of deep piety,
who loved Jesus Christ supremely and honored
Him as Savior and Lord. The monk's consistent
interest in them and his evident concern for their
personal salvation made a tremendous impres-
sion upon their hearts. Soon they prayed through
to spiritual reality—they were saved by the grace
of God, and they knew it.

When Will was 11, he joined his father in London and there formed a very close friendship with the minister of the church where they attended. Under this godly man's pastoral care, Will's calling to the ministry was firmly established in his heart.

When Frederick Bromley considered himself financially adequate to care for his children and begin a new life with them, he decided they should all migrate to Australia. They arrived in Melbourne on January 21, 1921, and proceeded to the country town of Mildura on the river Murray in northwestern Victoria. There Mr. Bromley soon obtained employment at his usual profession and became active, with his family, in the work of the Methodist Church.

Will was now in his midteens. His desire to serve the Lord was recognized by the church, so they granted him a local preacher's license. He was soon ministering in the small settlements in the surrounding country.

Under the influence of Rev. Thomas Indian, pastor of the Mildura Methodist Church, Will became acutely aware both of his need for "holiness of heart" and of a growing call to foreign missions. He realized that future service for God and the church, whether in Australia or abroad, would be mostly ineffective and seriously limited in fruitfulness unless he personally experienced the sin-purging baptism of the Holy Spirit. He therefore beseeched the Lord in prayer to make this experience real to him. Once it was obtained, he was determined to obey God on all points and at any cost.

About the year 1923, Will took a job as a striker in a blacksmith's shop at Mildura. Among several uncouth men who frequently came into the shop on business was one in particular who seemed to delight in ridiculing Will's faith and in using foul language. One day, Will accepted what seemed to be a providential opening to testify to the man about Christ's power to save. Later, this man's wife died, and he became very bitter against God. Will was soon at hand to express his sympathy, pray with him, and point him to the Savior, who could bring peace to his troubled heart. The man was soundly converted. A few years later in Melbourne, Will was instrumental in his joining the Methodist Church and becoming a lay leader in that fellowship.

Will purposed in his heart to be a soul winner, and he embraced each God-given opportunity to tell others about the Lord. In March of 1925, he enrolled in the Methodist Missionary Training College at Kew, a suburb of Melbourne. After graduation, he served as a pastor near Bendigo and in Ballarat and other places in Victoria. He also became engaged in city mission work in Adelaide, South Australia. During these years he still cherished the hope of someday being in foreign missionary service.

After a meeting with Japanese Christian leader Dr. Toyohiko Kagawa and reading some books by several missionaries to Japan, Will began to wonder if that country was to be his field of service. Wanting to be certain that this call was from God, he decided to go to the Torres Strait, north of Australia, where some Japanese pearling fleets were operating, find employment, and try to move among these people and witness to them. In all this, the hand of God was evident, for though Will eventually received a caution from God that Japan was not to be his field of labor, this move did put him in contact with the natives of the Torres islands, natives ethnically related to the people of New Guinea.

Will concluded his mission and returned to the mainland to serve in several successive pastorates in rural centers in Queensland. It is not clear how God finally assured him of his ultimate field of labor. Presumably during his sojourn in the Torres Strait islands, the spiritual needs of the multiplied thousands of New Guinea people not far from him to the north stirred his soul. God was doubtless conditioning the heart of His servant for a change in course, which found him, several months later, preparing for service in New Guinea with a settled conviction that the Lord was with him.

2

God's Guiding Hand

WILL LEFT QUEENSLAND to accept the pastorate of a small evangelical group in Melbourne, meanwhile praying for God's clear guidance concerning possible missionary service in New Guinea. He attended a missionary service one evening in Melbourne that was conducted by one of the directors of an independent "faith mission" operating at Pabarabuk in the New Guinea highlands. The inspiration of that service resulted in his joyful acceptance of an invitation to join the missionary staff of this group.

New Guinea, with an estimated population of 3 million, greatly challenged Will Bromley. He was now conscious of God's clear call to bring the gospel message to the primitive people who inhabited the highland regions, so he began at once to prepare for his new missionary assignment. After bidding farewell to his loved brother Clem and his many friends, he left Sydney by air for New Guinea early in the year 1950.

After undergoing customs formalities at Port Moresby (MOS-bee), Will flew on to Lae

(LAY) on the north coast. There he transferred to a light aircraft bound for Mount Hagen, in the Central Highlands. On arrival, Will was busy gathering his personal effects and enlisting native help to carry his load. He set out with his carriers to cover the first five miles of his journey to Pabarabuk by nightfall.

The following morning he was again on his way with his enlisted group of carriers to complete the remaining 20 miles of the journey. In the late afternoon, within sight of his destination, he was compelled to stop, exhausted after the hard day's walk over the rough, narrow trail. Between him and the mission station lay a ravine several hundred feet deep, with a fast flowing stream running through it. The tortuous trail running down its irregular sides, the turbulent stream, and the equally hazardous ascent on the far side convinced him he could go no further for the time being. While reflecting on his present predicament, a native warrior came to his aid. Will was soon on the back of this tough, sturdy highlander to be borne safely to the other side. In a short time he was at the Pabarabuk station, enjoying his favorite beverage—a good cup of hot tea.

Will settled zestfully into mission life and busied himself with many duties. He taught, rendered simple medical care, and indulged himself in the work he loved most—itinerant preaching. His humble bush dwelling was later shared by a colaborer, Bob Scott, who joined him from Australia in 1952. The men accepted as part of the

missionary life that they could see the stars at
night through holes in the grass thatch of the
roof. Bush rats and large cockroaches were con-
stant house companions.

Will's hobbies were beekeeping and flower
gardening. Wherever he traveled in the highlands, then, as in later years, there were beehives
and flowers. It was his custom often to scatter
flower seeds on mountainsides and in the valleys.

Despite being surrounded by such natural
beauty, Bob described the early days he and Will
spent together at Pabarabuk as "tense and nerve-
wracking at times." Axe, knife, and spear
wounds received by the natives in tribal fights
were common. In late 1952, a fight took place
right on the mission grounds in which one native
was killed and several wounded. The two men
did their best to minister to the bodies and souls
of those primitive savages whom, they believed,
God had entrusted to their care.

Will loved to tell the story of his first convert
at Pabarabuk. One of his houseboys had begun
to show unusual signs of distress, and it was
soon evident that he was under intense spiritual
conviction for having coveted and stolen a safety
pin, one of those ingenious devices of the "red"
man. With tender conscience, he had come to
Masta (Mr.) Bromley to make restitution and con-
fess his sins to God and ask His forgiveness.
While they prayed, the young man found his
way to Christ.

At the conclusion of Will's first term of service, he returned to Australia for furlough and to conduct deputation services. While there, he met several Nazarene preachers and laymen and was soon enjoying a close bond of fellowship with them. He read through the *Manual* of the denomination, found himself in agreement with it and, after much prayer, decided to join this holiness church with its aggressive, Calvary-centered missionary program.

After furlough, Will returned to Pabarabuk to carry on the work he had begun. News soon reached him that the Church of the Nazarene was contemplating launching missionary work in highland New Guinea. He at once began to seek the mind of the Lord about any contribution he might be able to make, as a Nazarene, to the church's proposed outreach in the territory. He had enjoyed his work at Pabarabuk and did not want to leave, yet he was sure in his own mind that he could more effectively serve God as a Nazarene missionary, with the church's solid organization and aggressive missionary program behind him, than by staying in any independent work with its attendant uncertainties. His major concern was to be at his best for God through the church with which he had cast his lot.

With the arrival of some new workers at Pabarabuk, Will soon became possessed by an undeniable assurance that God's ultimate plan for his life was in the process of being perfected. In this confidence, he decided to leave

Pabarabuk and return to Australia to await developments. In due course his formal application for missionary appointment was sent to the church headquarters in Kansas City. It was acknowledged, and there the matter stood.

The leaders of the Church of the Nazarene seemed hesitant to commit themselves concerning Will Bromley's application for service on the proposed New Guinea field. He was new to the church and unknown to its general leadership; and Will realized that caution on their part was wise and understandable, so he took a step of faith with the conviction that the Lord God was moving "the pillar of cloud" and he was following it in glad obedience.

He flew back to Australia, arriving in Brisbane on November 26, 1955, to accept the pastorate of the denomination's only aborigine church at Tweed Heads on the coast of northern New South Wales. He acquired some bees to keep him company and settled wholeheartedly into his new work for God and the church.

It did not seriously disturb him when, after 12 months' waiting, he received no response concerning his application. But after two years had gone by, and still no word had come, he occasionally began to wonder. However, on each occasion, he went directly to the place of prayer, always to rise from his knees strengthened in his faith and reassured. He would trust the Lord to order circumstances aright and unfold His plan at the proper time and in the best way. God had called him to serve in New Guinea as a Nazarene missionary, and he had no doubt about that call being fulfilled. It was "by faith and patience" that he would "inherit the promises."

It was to be almost three years before Will left Australia to take up his new missionary responsibilities at Kudjip in highland New Guinea. Meanwhile, he put heart and soul into the work at Tweed Heads, recognizing it to be an important part of God's overall plan for his life.

Finally the "silence" was broken. News reached him that General Superintendent Hardy C. Powers was planning to visit Australia and would preside at the district assembly in Brisbane in March of 1957. Dr. Powers desired to interview him at that time concerning his application for missionary service.

Will told his story at length and explained how God had led him to the Church of the Nazarene and had called him to New Guinea. He let it be known that, with all his heart, he wanted to serve in the highlands among primitive peoples and to engage in the work he loved most—itinerant evangelism. He would be willing and content to serve until retirement or death without furlough.

Many questions were asked, all of which were satisfactorily answered. Then one particular question was raised, the gist of which was: "Brother Bromley, it is not our policy to appoint single men to the mission field. Have you any special reason for remaining a single man?"

Will replied: "Well, dear brother, I did have a sweet, Christian, young lady. We loved each other very much and planned to marry and go to the mission field together, but it pleased the Lord to take her home to heaven. I have not yet found anyone who could fill her place in my life."

There were tears, and there was perfect understanding. During the district assembly that followed, amid scenes of great rejoicing, Will was one of four men ordained to elders' orders by Dr. Powers.

Plans were at last completed for Will's assignment to New Guinea. In the providence of God, he left Brisbane on the ship *Bulolo,* destined for Madang on New Guinea's north coast. Many people came to the riverside wharf at Brisbane to say good-bye, including a large group of members and friends from the Tweed Heads Church, 65 miles to the south.

Will was able to take a motorbike with him to use on the highland trails, thanks to the generosity of the Australian District Nazarene World Mission Society. He also took his bees with him and even gave them a "fly" at Port Moresby. He arrived at Madang on August 12, 1958, and shortly took off by air for the mission station at Kudjip in the Wahgi Valley.

On August 30, Will wrote from Kudjip:

This is a land of great opportunity to proclaim the gospel, and also a challenge to our faith. We on the field do so much appreciate your prayers. And when we look upon this land and see thousands without the gospel, living in heathen darkness, we can truly say: "The harvest truly is plenteous, but the labourers are few; pray ye therefore the Lord of the harvest, that he will send forth labourers into his harvest" (Matthew 9:37-38). I am personally grateful for all the love and prayers of Nazarenes in Australia, and the kind messages sent to me as I embarked on the ship for New Guinea. I am also grateful to all at our Headquarters in the United States and the many unseen friends who have been, and still are, praying for me.

The Wahgi

THE COOL, DELIGHTFUL Wahgi valley, which is 5,500 feet above sea level, runs generally southeast to northwest for at least 100 miles and is about 20 miles wide. It is bounded by the cloud-topped peaks of the Kubor (KOO-bo) Range to the south and the Schrader (SRAY-da) Ranges to the north. It rains heavily almost every night in the Wahgi, but the days are mostly fine. The deep blue skies patched with fleecy clouds allow for generally good flying conditions.

I accompanied General Superintendent Powers into this populous valley early in December 1954 on an investigative tour for the church. Our introduction to this "new world" of spiritual need was as depressing as it was exciting. It was at once concluded that something had to be done to bring the gospel to those lost people, and it had to be done soon. Dr. Powers' burden for these highlanders found expression in his book *And Now New Guinea*, which intensified the interest that had already been aroused in the church.

The Nazarene World Mission Society had already celebrated its 40th anniversary by arranging a "Hallelujah March" Offering on Sunday, June 20, 1954, to raise money to help establish missionary work in New Guinea. The astounding response was an amount over $100,000. Now with Dr. Powers' firsthand report on the proposed new field, arrangements were soon under way to send the church's first missionary couple to enter this wide-open door.

Sidney and Wanda Knox, with their infant son, Geron, arrived in Port Moresby on October 14, 1955. After Sidney had made an exploratory tour of the highlands, they decided to settle in the Wahgi valley at a placed called Kudjip. Sidney got busy with an aggressive building program, and after several weeks a church building and mission house were completed. It was not long before he had organized his first day school with an enrollment in excess of 50 young people, most of whom were boys. Among the first pupils was a smiling lad of about 10 years named Ap, of whom we shall hear more later.

Less than three years after the Knoxes arrived in New Guinea, Sidney's health had seriously deteriorated. This necessitated their return to the United States for him to receive specialized treatment. Sidney did not recover from this illness, and it pleased the Lord to take him home to heaven. Wanda later returned to the field with their children, Geron and Janie, to carry on nobly the work she and her husband had so fruitfully begun.

Meanwhile, Rev. and Mrs. Max Condor and

their children had arrived in Kudjip from the United States to give help and direction to the work. When Will Bromley joined them, these three missionaries comprised the only Nazarene workforce in New Guinea.

Will undertook his missionary work with typical commitment. He pastored a native church at Kowi, about four miles from Kudjip, and taught second grade in school during the week. His years of experience with highland natives plus his ready ability with the pidgin (neo-Melanesian) language made him a particularly valuable asset. Once he had established his bee-hives and flower gardens, he considered himself completely settled in.

The new missionary had become intrigued by the boy Ap. He eyed him constantly with prophetic interest, thinking within himself: Here is a lad with ability and promise for future service in the work of the Lord. Ap adopted Will as a second father almost immediately after they had become acquainted.

Much attention was now being focused on the Jimi Valley, a vast mountainous region that lay two days' walk north from Kudjip over rough, arduous trails. A government patrol post had just been established at a place called Tabibuga in order to bring under control this recently discovered part of the territory with its thousands of primitive people. Plans for the peaceful penetration of the unexplored part of the valley were now being pushed ahead.

The conviction had been deepening with Will Bromley and Max Condor that the time was ripe for the mission to widen the scope of its influence to include the Jimi Valley. As far as Will was personally concerned, this was the one place in the world above all others where he wanted to serve God. The prospect excited him and fitted in perfectly with what he believed was his God-assigned task—to live among untouched, primitive people, win their confidence, and lead them to the Lord Jesus Christ. So, early in the year 1959, Max and Will set out hopefully for the long walk into the Jimi to investigate the possibilities for locating a site and establishing a mission there. Halfway there, however, they were forced to turn back due to circumstances surrounding the construction of a new airstrip at Tabibuga.

About the middle of the year, Will decided to make another try. With two mission boys, Napil and Taimil, he eagerly set out on his journey. Late on the second day he reached the Tabibuga patrol post to be warmly welcomed by *Kiap* (Patrol Officer) Barry Ryan, who courteously offered him hospitality for the night. He also made available the services of a native interpreter named Peri to help him with his contacts in the valley.

After an early start on the new day, Will and his three helpers entered the main part of the valley. It was green, rugged country, unspoiled by the marks of modern civilization. At each turn on the mountainsides, new vistas held Will en-

thralled, and he loved every minute of it. Excitedly he journeyed on until he came to a place
called Tsingoropa (sing-GO-row-po), where a
beautiful stream plunged recklessly downward.
Here Will stopped awhile, charmed by the music
of its waters.

Close by was an area covered by tall trees
and thick jungle undergrowth, which, at first
sight, appeared to offer good possibilities for a
mission location. In writing about this event later, Will stated:

> I sat down and considered what I could
> make of it when the jungle was cleared. I
> then went on to Kwibin [KWEE-pn], which
> was on top of a high mountain: No suitable
> place for building, no water, the road too
> mountainous for carrying cargo, and too far
> from the airstrip. Back I came to Tsingoropa
> and looked the place over again, prayed
> about it, and called out for the chief of the
> tribe.

In fact, Will met several chiefs in the valley on
this day, but no definite arrangement for the ac-
quisition of property could be made. The tribal
leaders were nervous and distrustful of the
stranger.

As the evening closed in and the cloud cover
intensified, Will and his helpers made their way
back to Tabibuga for the night, and from there to
Karap, Banz, and finally Kudjip. He arrived at
the main station fired with enthusiasm and not
altogether disappointed because of his failure to

make a property deal. Maybe the time was not yet ripe, but with the assurance that God's clock keeps perfect time, he prayed on and waited hopefully.

About 12 months after Will's arrival on the field, the small missionary group was joined by Wallace and Mona White and their young sons, Rob and Steve, from the United States. Wallace and Mona soon began to add strength and inspiration to that which had already been accomplished in and around Kudjip.

* * * * *

It was early November 1959, and Will's first field vacation was overdue. Ap, who by this time had become a Christian, wanted Masta Bromley to spend this period at Tun (TOON), his home area, 12 miles west of the Kudjip station. Will was anxious to cultivate Ap's friendship still further; and being hopeful of extending the church's influence to the Tun area, he gladly accepted the invitation. Mountain, jungle, and stream were fascinating to him, but to be with these new people was the superior delight. He ate with them, talked with them about his wonderful Savior, and lived at ease among them until a secure bond of friendship was formed between them and the mission Will was representing. From this time onward, Will and Ap, now about 13 years of age, became inseparable friends.

Will and Wallace often talked to each other about the church's proposed outreach into the Jimi Valley. They decided that the best time to enter this area would be immediately after the airstrip at Tabibuga, which had been under construction for almost two years, had been declared operational.

Will prayed earnestly and often that God would soon give the church an open door to the Jimi. He and Wallace knew that the airstrip was shortly to be approved for traffic, so they arranged with the Missionary Aviation Fellowship to fly them into Tabibuga as soon as the authorities gave them clearance. Meanwhile, Will and Wallace remained prayerfully on the alert.

The Jimi

AT LAST THE WELCOME word came that the Tabibuga airstrip was to be opened to light aircraft on Monday, December 28, 1959. Will and Wallace had been in frequent touch with their friend, MAF Pilot Max Flavell, who at once agreed to fly them into the valley.

The two men took off from the Banz airstrip early in the morning on this exciting day. Within 20 minutes, they landed on the new field, touching down not many minutes after a government official's plane had left and just after the strip had been declared operational. Theirs was the second plane to land there. The plane was soon unloaded, and after arranging with the pilot to be back at Tabibuga late the following afternoon, they set about the task of finding and organizing a line of carriers to handle their cargo.

Their destination was Kwibin, a range summit, located about 10 miles away. After covering about 3 miles, they came to Wata Tonga, where a pretty waterfall shed its cold contents down the mountainside to feed a rocky stream that cut across the main trail. This stream formed part of the tribal boundary between the Warames (WAH-rah-mess) and Tsingoropa peoples. Here the carriers downed their loads, refusing to go any further. Tribal taboos and deeply entrenched enmities were the cause of their reluctance to proceed, so they were at once paid off.

A few yards ahead, the trail led into the Tsingoropa area through an opening in a kind of picket fence. The pointed stakes on either side were liberally covered with a mixture of pigs' blood and paint pigment. Once through the opening and into Tsingoropa territory, the missionaries began to shout for helpers. A few recruits emerged from the bush, and the men were again on their way.

They journeyed along the rugged way and before long passed by Tsingoropa. Here Will cast a hopeful eye on the piece of property he had coveted for the mission on his hurried visit six months before.

They turned in a northwesterly direction up a steep, zigzag trail. Again they came to a tribal boundary where, as before, their carriers lowered their burdens and refused to continue. More carriers were hired, but the other men followed behind. However, they would not venture through any of the tribal gates they encountered. Instead, they made wide detours and rejoined the trail farther on. They felt that if the tribal taboos were bypassed, immunity against witchcraft and sorcery was assured; but if they passed through these blood-smeared entrances, they would soon fall prey to the evil spirits who guarded them.

The men sent a runner on ahead to Kwibin with a request that the *luluai* (LOO-loo-ah-ee, the supreme chief) or *tultul* (the subordinate chief) of that area meet them at the summit. However, after speaking with these tribal leaders and receiving little positive response, they made their way back to Tsingoropa.

After praying for God's guidance, Will called out for the local *luluai*. A man named Alu ventured forth to greet them and listened with evident interest to their story about the mission and what they hoped it could do for his people. They were standing together on the coveted piece of property, but Will thought it best not to ask the chief directly for it. Instead, he inquired whether Alu could suggest a suitable site for the proposed mission, if, in the chief's mind, he would be welcome to come and live in this area. Alu eyed him appraisingly, then smiled and said: "You can have the ground we are standing on." Although inwardly delighted, Will replied with studied outward casualness: "It is rather small, but it will do."

With the support of four native men, Will and Wallace cut their way around a block of three and a half acres. When they got back to the main trail, they hacked out a clearing at the base of four large yar trees, where they were able to pitch their tent and camp for the night.

They were up early the next morning to take a much more careful look at the property. They

found to their intense satisfaction that the
ground was as level as could be expected in the
Jimi. The location was at a main trail junction,
with the clear Tsingoropa stream flowing nearby.
In addition, they were enjoying the good will of
the *luluai*, without which no real progress could
be made. It was hoped, too, that Alu, sometime
in the future, would make an adjoining piece of
property available as the growing needs of the
proposed mission station demanded.

Deeply grateful that God had so evidently answered prayer and prospered their journey, they
emerged from this densely wooded wonderland
about the middle of the afternoon and made their
way to Tabibuga, where, as arranged, the MAF
plane picked them up and flew them back to Banz.

Before the end of January 1960, Will and Wallace again entered the Jimi. They proceeded directly to the Tsingoropa site to salute Alu and to enlist
help to cut enough of the jungle away for the erection of the first of the mission buildings. Through
the good offices of this *luluai*, willing hands were
soon at work. As soon as the clearing operation
was completed, the men returned to Kudjip to pursue their appointed tasks. Now Max Condor's only
condition for Will to enter the Jimi permanently
was that certain critical work at the main station be
completed first; then he would be free to go.

* * * * *

On August 5, 1960, Will and Ap flew from
Banz into Tabibuga and arrived at Tsingoropa to

take up permanent residence. Within an hour, the tent had been erected and the camp set up on a spot that had been neatly cleared for them by local natives. Will wrote to Wallace: "Alu is a great chap and cannot do enough to care for us in every way, and always has that very nice smile of his."

Fourteen years old, Ap was jubilant at being able to serve with Will in the Jimi Valley. Their relationship was one of deep mutual attachment. Will found in Ap an efficient young man of many arts and parts; he served as houseboy, store boy, cook, barber, and interpreter. In the latter capacity he excelled, having acquired the Jimi dialect speedily and efficiently. In Will's view, this boy was God's special gift to him for this new pioneering enterprise.

By the end of the month, Wallace and three other men from the Wahgi flew into the Jimi to help Will with the erection of the framework of the mission house. As before, one group of carriers transported the cargo to Wata Tonga, where it was taken over by an excited and enthusiastic band of Tsingoropa volunteers, who, with Missionary Bromley, had been anticipating the arrival of the entourage. Let Wallace continue to describe the scene:

> Excitement was running high. The carriers were singing out in native fashion to let the others know we were approaching. As we drew near, the natives began the chant which accompanies an attack. They would rush for-

ward, then fall back a few paces, only to re-
peat the process again. Then all together they
began to sing out, "Whooo-ahhhhh!" holding
the same pitch and increasing the volume to
an earsplitting crescendo. We could hear the
response of the natives in the camp.

When we stepped into the clearing,
there were about 150 natives clearing the
station site of jungle undergrowth. Our first
task was to build a mission home out of native materials . . . The church and other
buildings were to follow.

Wallace remained with Will until the house
site had been leveled and the framework posi-
tioned. He then left him and Ap to continue on
with the work, assisted by the other helpers from
the Wahgi. The government, through the *Kiap* at
Tabibuga, courteously released 120 men who had
been working on the completion of the airstrip to
assist with the clearing and building operations
at Tsingoropa.

With this added help, the live jungle quickly
yielded to the work of the cutters until the con-
tours of the site became apparent. A wide shoulder on the range side was revealed that, after
sloping gradually for a few hundred yards, fell
away sharply to a lower complexity of gullies
and scrubby undergrowth. Will's plan was to
transform this wilderness into three broad ter-
races, to include locations for mission buildings,
lawns, and gardens.

Tent life in the jungle was giving Will close

personal contact with many of the people. He was gradually winning the confidence of the men, and Alu was maintaining a friendly attitude, although still unwilling to make any extra property available to the mission. The *tultul*, Guan, had also made Will's acquaintance and appeared to be favorably impressed with the newcomer.

However, it was not until Mona White came in from Kudjip for a weekend to be with her husband on one of his visits that the native women overcame their shyness to meet the missionaries. Mona's loving disposition and gracious way with the women dispelled their fears, and from that time onward there was no hesitancy on their part to hear what the missionary had to say or to bring food for sale to help feed the workers on the station.

Right from the inception of his work in this area, Will lost no opportunity to witness to the people about Christ, but his words and stories sounded strange in the ears of these lost individuals who had not the slightest concept of a loving God, much less the redemptive work of His Son. Will could see that it would have to be "precept upon precept; line upon line . . . here a little, and there a little" in his teaching ministry until God's arrows of conviction would be able to penetrate their hearts.

Will had not been long in the area when he planned his first public service. In his mind, he wondered how he should approach the people

with the message of the gospel, and he prayed
about the matter until he sensed an answer from
the Holy Spirit. He gathered a group of people
and arranged for them to sit under the trees in
the new clearing. He began the service by playing some recordings; then he prayed and
preached, with Ap interpreting.

He took a little seed to illustrate his first
message. Here is an excerpt from a taped interview given by Will during his first furlough in
Australia, illustrating this important occasion:

> I remember the first time, when I held
> my first church service. I had to consider
> just how I could present the message to
> them. I thought it would be a good idea if I
> took a seed and just told them that this seed
> has life in it; and when they planted this
> seed, it would grow and develop and pro-
> duce fruit. I told these people that they
> could not make a seed like they made an axe
> or a bow and arrow and spear, etc. I said to
> them: "Do you think your ancestors could
> make this seed?" and of course they knew
> very well that it was impossible . . .
>
> They attribute so much of their calami-
> ties to evil spirits or the spirits of their ances-
> tors. They think that when trouble comes
> along, they have offended their ancestors,
> who are thus cross with them and therefore
> bring these calamities upon them. While
> they do believe that the spirits of their ances-
> tors can bless them in some ways, it seems

to us that there are more curses than blessings meted out by them. Therefore we say: "Now your ancestors could not make this seed. You had to make your axe, you had to make your bows, you had to make your arrows, and what have you.

"Well, we believe . . . that we have a Father, a Supreme Being, whom we call God, who made all things. The good things that we have given to us such as food, and the sun, moon, stars, and the rain that comes down, all these have been made and given to us by God." They see that it is reasonable from their point of view, because they have to depend so much upon natural things.

In this clear and interesting manner, Will talked about God and then went on to explain about the Bible. Then he proceeded to tell them in the simplest of terms the story of the cross of Christ and God's plan of redemption. Thus interest was awakened and regular services, in this humble way, began to be a part of the way of life in and around Tsingoropa.

Laying Foundations

BY LATE SEPTEMBER, Will was living in his neat little bush cottage. By the end of October, Wallace was back at Tsingoropa to help Will put the finishing touches to the construction. The church building, with a seating capacity of 500, had also been completed. Like the cottage, it had a grass thatch roof, pitpit walls, and a woven bamboo floor. There were no pews, but a platform with benches had been installed, and a pulpit—Jimi Valley style. About this time, Will established his beehives and flower gardens as well.

Will's days were full and demanding. He worked from daylight until dark, giving direction to the work, preaching to small groups, and witnessing here and there. Throughout the day, he was always available to help those who needed medical attention. He kept his medical books handy and also a good supply of penicillin, salves, and medicines. People were brought to him from as far as two days' walk away to have pig bites, cerebral malaria, tropical ulcers and skin diseases, conjunctivitis, and other ills cared for.

Will had to battle not only disease but also ignorance, superstition, and, at times, blatant deviltry. But he undertook his varied missionary assignments with the deep conviction that he was personally indebted to these people. The fact that he genuinely loved them could not be hidden. The people were recognizing that this kind, smiling red man who had come to live in their midst had no ulterior motives. He was here to give them *God's tok,* which he declared could change their lives just as it had changed his own.

For many weeks Will had keenly anticipated that happy occasion when he would preach to his first congregation inside the new Tsingoropa church building. Multiplied scores of people had promised to come, including Alu and Guan, who had given their word not only that they would be there themselves but also that their tribal lines (families) would be well represented. Will had made ready for this service by much prayer and personal preparation of heart as well as careful planning of the message he would give.

There were very few signs of activity around the station that morning; and when service time had come, only a handful of people had arrived. Will and Ap went inside the church with the portable record player and waited. It was soon evident that all who intended to be at church that morning were already there, so Will proceeded with the service as God gave him grace and understanding. This over, he asked himself the tantalizing question: What has gone wrong? After some deep thought, he decided to find Alu to try to uncover the cause of the problem.

Will climbed the mountainside, and in no more than half an hour he had reached the *luluai's* hut. He found him home and quite ready to talk. "Alu," Will began, "you promised me that you and Guan and your people would be at church this morning. Why have you not come? Is anything wrong?" Alu lost no time with his blunt rejoinder: "There is a rumor around the bush that you are here only for one thing—you want to change our tribal customs, which have been handed down to us by our ancestors. We do not want our customs changed, so that is why I and my people were not at church this morning. Furthermore, we do not ever intend to go to church."

Will had known long before that the prince of darkness would challenge the mission's penetration of this part of his realm, and so he was not unduly surprised at such a development. Immediately, he lifted his heart in prayer, knowing that he needed God's wisdom in his answer.

God surely spoke as Will replied, "Alu, you have broken a promise. Up to now, I have known you to be fair and a man of your word. What surprises me is that you have listened to rumors in the bush and on these made your decision not to come to church. I now invite you to come and hear *God's tok* next Sunday morning. You will then be able to hear and judge for yourself if these stories are worth listening to and whether you consider what you have heard to be right or wrong." Alu's respect for Will overcame his fears, for the time being at least, so he promised to attend church the following Sunday.

The missionary waited at church the next Sunday with the calm confidence that God had heard and answered the earnest prayers he had been praying all week. Men, women, and children, many of them newcomers, were filing into the new building while Will greeted them cordially at the door. It was especially gratifying to welcome Alu, who, true to his promise, had come to hear and judge for himself. At the conclusion of the service, Will sensed there was a greater freedom between him and the people as he moved among them.

Whatever Alu's exact opinions were during that service, no one knows, except that he seemed to feel that *Masta* Bromley's message contained nothing but good, and obviously the missionary had the best interests of his people at heart. From this time onward, no difficulty was experienced in getting the people to attend church.

It was not many weeks after this first episode that Alu and Guan, early on a certain Sunday, visited the station to inform Will that they and their tribal lines would not be at church that morning. A young relative of theirs had suddenly passed away. The two chiefs, wrapped up in their sorrow, wanted to explain to Will ahead of time the reason for their intended absence and to promise to be at church the following Sunday. Will listened to their sad story and said: "I, too, have known this kind of sorrow and offer my deep sympathy to you both." Thereupon the chiefs broke down and wept.

The following Sunday, during the service, Will made public mention of the bereavement. While so doing, he was emotionally overcome himself. At the conclusion of the service one of the chiefs spoke to Ap, who was standing by: "How could the *Masta* feel so upset? He is not of our color." Ap replied, "Don't you know the *Masta* loves us all and wants to see us all go to heaven when we die? He feels that so many of us will go to hell if we do not change our ways; therefore he is moved with love for us." This incident overwhelmingly convinced Alu that Will's love for him and his people was beyond question, and from that time the chief and the missionary became very close friends.

A day school had by now been established with about 50 boys enrolled. Will planned to bring these lads through to the second grade, at which time those who qualified would be encouraged to enroll at Kudjip for the higher grades.

By the turn of the year Mininga, whom Wallace had hired from the patrol officer, had been added to the staff. This boy also had a good working knowledge of pidgin and thus was well able to serve Will at the Tsingoropa station as cargo line *boss boi.*

The seeds of truth were continually being sown but, so far, without any visible sign of fruitfulness. However, Will rested on God's wonderful promise: "He that goeth forth and weepeth, bearing precious seed, shall doubtless come again with rejoicing, bringing his sheaves with him" (Psalm 126:6).

General Superintendent Samuel Young and Mrs. Young included New Guinea in a planned administrative tour of the southwest Pacific early in 1961. It was arranged for Dr. Young to visit this rugged missionary outpost at Tsingoropa and spend a couple of days with Will.

Will took the opportunity to give Dr. Young a firsthand report of his work and a clear concept of his burden and aspirations for a spiritual awakening. It distressed him deeply that he was unable to report at least one convert during this first year on the new field. They talked on into the night over a pot of tea, the general superintendent listening with characteristic sympathy and understanding.

The next day the schoolboys were assembled for the receiving of awards. Dr. Young looked on and shared in the proceedings and then trekked the five miles back to the airstrip. Within a month of Dr. and Mrs. Young's visit to the field, Rev. and Mrs. Max Condor and family concluded their term of service and returned to America. Wallace was then given the responsibility of mission leadership.

* * * * *

On November 7, 1961, Miss Margaret Robson arrived at Kudjip from Australia to give direction to the medical work, which, at that time, was in its early stages of development. Margaret had gained a triple certificate in nursing (general nursing, midwifery, and child welfare) and had also graduated from the Nazarene Bible College in Sydney. She brought to the field several years of wide experience in nursing and a deep sense of commitment to the task to which she believed God had called her.

Little did Margaret realize that, scarcely two years hence, she was to become Mrs. William Bromley and would share in the joyful experience of a divine visitation in the spiritually dark Jimi Valley.

Visiting Tsingoropa

I HAD ARRIVED at Goroka (go-ROW-ka) in the central highlands early Sunday morning, March 25, 1962. Wallace was there with an MAF plane to meet me, and soon we were on our way to Banz, nearest airstrip (at that time) to Kudjip, where I was to speak in the morning service. This was my third trip to New Guinea and the beginning of nine delightful days of preaching and visiting in the Wahgi.

It was a special joy to greet the new Christians, 31 of whom had recently been baptized and publicly confessed Christ. One could not help but contrast this happy scene with that depressing one I saw in this very locality eight years previously. All seemed darkness and despair for the people of the Wahgi then—now there was light and hope.

Margaret had just taken over three welfare clinics from the government and opened a fourth. She was also in charge of the *haus-sick*, a simple clinic-hospital constructed with native materials and seldom without patients. These outlets for her medical skill—with the help of three *doktabois* ("doctor boys")—kept her busy and provided many opportunities to witness for Christ.

* * * * *

It was April 6, 1962, a day that had been long and keenly anticipated. Wallace and I were to visit Will in the Jimi and spend several days with him. As soon as the morning rain cleared, we piled our baggage into the mission jeep and made our way to the Banz strip, five miles distant, arriving there about seven o'clock.

After the usual weather delays and a few tense moments, we made it to Tabibuga. As we climbed out of the plane, Will was nowhere to be seen, but Wallace, who never appeared to be lost in any emergency, found a way to get in touch with him. We saw atop a nearby hill a native warrior, silhouetted against the sky. Wallace cupped his hands and shouted a message. The man caught on and relayed the message to another point of contact on another hill, and so on. Within 20 minutes a message had come back to us, via the same medium, that Will was coming along the trail with his carriers. When he arrived, we exchanged greetings and chatted awhile before setting out for the Tsingoropa station.

The deeply worn trail that was now so familiar to Will and Wallace was to me new and exciting. News travels fast in the bush; and as we trudged along, groups of people were already gathered here and there along the trail to greet the visitor. These almost naked people had the usual pig's fat applied to their bodies. Some adorned their faces with black, grated charcoal, while others included facial paint, sometimes in a variety of colors. Others sported various combinations of feathered headgear, woven armbands, possum fur, and other kinds of fetishes. Not a few came up to touch an arm or shoulder, give a pat on the back, or feel the texture of our clothing. These familiarities were sometimes followed by merry peals of laughter, and occasionally by the native way of expressing excited amazement: the wringing of the hands, simultaneously with the high-pitched squeal, "Ahhhhheeeeee!" We frequently heard the greeting: "*Apinoon, Masta*" ("Good afternoon, Sir").

We paused to admire the view of the mission station from atop the mountain. As I turned to resume the trek, my attention was arrested by a native man moving quickly in my direction. It soon became clear (for I had been warned) that he was about to express a friendly greeting in the native manner. He hugged me with both arms, rubbed his whiskers on my face, smiled generously, and then retired to the bush. It was his way of saying, "Greetings and grace," but what I actually received was "gratings and grease." There was something about this genial fellow that really rubbed off on me! My guess is that it was a mixture of rancid pig's fat and charcoal. Will stood there grinning broadly at my wide-eyed surprise, and I think I detected certain physical vibrations about him that suggested that he was "killing himself laughing" on the inside. This, incidentally, was only one of many similar greetings expressed and dutifully received.

We arrived at Tsingoropa in the early afternoon and were soon surrounded by a crowd of inquisitive but friendly people. Alu and Guan were there, also Chiefs Indama and Nyinga (NING-ah) from a nearby area. Koroma (KOR-ma) had come from Kwibin, suffering from a heavy chest cold and quite ready to trust Will's medicine. Alu, whose vanity was served by a liberal application of charcoal on his face and patches of bright blue on forehead and nose, saluted us in breezy style.

Almost every evening, when all was quiet in the surrounding jungle, we talked well into the night over the usual pot of tea. Will was an ardent conversationalist; and once he got on to a favorite subject such as the native people and their culture, the amazing habits of the bee, Albert Schweitzer, Toyohiko Kagawa, or, more particularly, the longed-for spiritual awakening in the Jimi, there was no holding him back. In slow, smiling conversation, he would often carry on late into the night, while hopefully cooperative listeners would nod on the borderline of sleep. I sometimes wondered if Will concluded that these were nods of assent and so became fired up to continue the conversation. Anyway, this was a part of the pleasure of knowing Will, for his talks were always informative and enriching—at least until heavy eyelids took over. Surprisingly, he would be up early the next morning with his usual physical vigor to care for the duties of the day.

Early on the day following our arrival, scores of natives began to seat themselves on the lawn outside the mission cottage. They had their bows, arrows, spears, stone axes, and other accessories, obviously intent on impressing the visitor. A few were shy and retiring and looked us over from a distance, but most of them took a closer look and offered to shake hands in European style.

We went out on the lawn to greet Chiefs Alu, Guan, Indama, Nyinga, Koroma, and Ninimp (nee-NIMP), each of whom wore on his forehead a brass badge of office supplied by the Australian government. Will kept looking at me for my reaction. I couldn't miss it—he loved these men and coveted them for Christ. They were **his** people.

It took the greater part of the day to receive gifts from the *luluais* and *tultuls* and one or two others, each having brought a live chicken with their best wishes and respects. There was voluminous speech making by each one, paying tribute to Will and the mission, and making it clear that these gifts of appreciation were genuine—no strings attached. (However, less than a week had gone by before Will was asked for favors in recognition of the generosity to the visitor from Australia!)

One of the highlights of my visit was a feast and general get-together arranged by Wallace and Will to be held on the main lawn of the mission station. It was to be a gesture of appreciation to the chiefs and their people for lending willing hands to clear the jungle and excavate the ground for the Tsingoropa station. Wallace had a sizable supply of canned beef and several large bags of rice brought in for the occasion. Pigs, donated by the chiefs and people, were cooked in the native fashion—in a pit. The rice was boiled in large gasoline drums.

By late afternoon a great crowd of men and women, boys and girls were seated on the wide lawn, each supplied with a piece of banana leaf to serve as a platter. The chiefs served the food, each person receiving a piece of roast pork, some *kau kau* (sweet potatoes, their staple food), beef, and rice. The chiefs reserved large portions for themselves, befitting their office. It was a great occasion for the Jimi people.

After the jungle banquet was over, and as the darkness deepened, Alu, Koroma, and others made long speeches, expressing gratitude for the Nazarene mission and bragging about the beautiful station in their midst. It being Saturday, each one urged—almost conscripted—his people to go to church on the morrow.

I stood alone on a hillside not far from the middle terrace to watch the proceedings. The sky was overcast with not a star to be seen, and this intensified the blackness of the night. By the light of an open fire, I could see Will in the thick of things with Wallace, Ap, and Mininga. The time had come at last for the people to leave for their homes. One by one they came to light their dry bamboo torches from the fire to guide their feet over dark trails on their homeward journey. Some were lighting theirs from others already burning. Then, in small family groups, they began to walk away from the station in all directions—many hundreds of them. It was an unforgettable sight.

As my vigil wore on, I began to wonder: Could this be prophetic? I think I waited for more than an hour before the last spot of light seemed to extinguish. I shared Will's hope for that day when the spiritual fire he had hoped to light at Tsingoropa would spread out into the dark recesses of the Jimi jungle. I walked to where Will was standing and commented on the fascinating sight of the lighted torches receding into the blackness of the jungle night. I cannot recall that he replied. He just stood there, obviously in deep thought, which I was not disposed to interrupt.

* * * * *

It was now Sunday. People could be seen early in the morning sauntering along the trails leading to the Tsingoropa church. By midmorning they were moving into the church building to take whatever places appealed to them, which was right up front for the first-comers. The women took their places on the right and the men on the left. All squatted on the bamboo floor in haphazard formation.

When the service was about to begin, we walked down an irregular semblance of an aisle, with the press of seminaked bodies on either side, to take our places on the platform. Will commenced by playing a few recordings, then prayed in pidgin with Ap interpreting. There was a period of chorus singing, each chorus being sung three times. Wallace had something to say; then Will made an introduction, after which certain chiefs interrupted to pass on their comments. After this, I was called on to deliver the message. I spoke in English, which Will translated into pidgin, and Ap then translated into the local language—"turn talk twice." The whole service lasted between two and three hours. At the close, several hands were raised in response to an appeal. Whether this public expression was just a gesture of goodwill to the visitor or the beginnings of a work of God in their hearts, we could not exactly determine.

* * * * *

The morning of my departure came, and with much reluctance I packed my belongings and bade farewell to many newfound friends. Will was to accompany Wallace and me back to Kudjip as he had a top-priority appointment with the missionary nurse, Margaret Robson, coming up at the main station. We climbed the ridge to meet the main trail and made our way toward the airstrip. Passing by Malkaba, we paused to speak with Kena, *luluai* of the Warames, about the possibility of establishing a mission among his people. His response was noncommittal, so we let the matter drop for the time being and resumed our hike. After an hour of waiting for the pilot to find a break in the clouds, we boarded the plane and left the fertile valley below us.

"It's Coming, Dear Brother;
I Know It's Coming"

BEFORE WILL RETURNED to Tsingoropa, he
and Margaret announced their engagement to be
married. They had both previously prayed
through on this important decision, believing it
to be the will of God for their lives. They hoped
it would be an added asset to the church's outreach in the Jimi Valley, where, as a husband-
and-wife team, they could serve the Lord more
effectively.

* * * * *

Will's concern for a great spiritual awakening in the Jimi was now being intensified to the
point of protracted seasons of burdened intercession. It had been his joy over the last two years to
preach and witness to these people, but he concluded it was high time he should be seeing
some conspicuous conversions to Christ. There
had been a few marginal professions of faith in
Christ, but no genuine conversions evidenced by

a change of living. Even Ap, his faithful helper, had slipped and later married a heathen girl from his home area of Tun. This must have caused Will untold grief even though Ap, still deeply devoted to Will, continued to help with the work. However, the missionary's hope was in God, and he steadfastly believed that the Holy Spirit would surely bring a spiritual awakening into the Jimi in spite of the apparent setbacks.

Moreover, God did not leave Will Bromley without some very real encouragements. Alu had, with ever deepening devotion to Will, at last agreed to release another five and a half acres to the mission, thus making a total of nine acres. Then Kena, the *luluai* from Warames, with his *tultul*, Konch (KONS), offered to sell some property to the mission after seeing the mission's work at Kudjip. Koroma and Ninimp had also made land available at Kwibin, so the influence of the church was being appreciably extended. Finally, the Australian District NWMS had, by the beginning of 1963, pledged enough money to erect a dispensary building at Tsingoropa, providing a place for Margaret to work when she joined Will in the Jimi to take over the medical work.

Will's first furlough was about due. He sought approval to make it an abbreviated one, and this being granted, he left for Australia to be there in time for the district assembly, at Margate, Queensland, early in March 1963. After some deputation work in his homeland, he

sailed for England on April 8 to speak in the
churches in the British Isles and to visit his sister,
Betsy, for a while.

He returned to Australia in August, and he
and Margaret were married in the College
Church of the Nazarene in Thornleigh, Sydney,
on September 7. So, after only six months' absence, Will arrived back at his loved Tsingoropa
with his bride to occupy a nice new cottage that
Wallace had erected for them in his absence to replace the old bush one, now demolished.

Each morning a group of sick people could
be seen outside the consulting room of the dispensary. Men and women, old and young, waited their turn for "the missus" to diagnose their
ailments, administer medicine, and, with the aid
of her *doktaboi*, give injections and apply ban-
dages. A few stayed on for the care of more serious ills. Her service of healing was binding more
and more people to the mission, thus, in turn, increasing church attendance. In addition, Will was
being released to perform the important duties of
his preaching and teaching ministries.

It was June 1966 when I again visited the Jimi, this time accompanied by my wife, Marion.
During this visit we found Will undergoing an
earnest and intense self-evaluation as he re-
viewed his six years' work in the Jimi. **He could
not name even one soul won to Christ in that
period.** He opened his heart to the close scrutiny
of God's Spirit in the light of Psalm 139:23—
"Search me, O God, and know my heart." It was

a favorite text of his and one heavily under-
scored in his Bible and rewritten in the margin.
He emerged from this season of soul-searching
renewed in his faith and encouraged. He would
say: "The revival is coming, dear brother; I **know**
it's coming."

* * * * *

John William Bromley was born on April 27,
1966. His coming to the Bromley home had pro-
voked much praise to God from very grateful
parents. Margaret's health had not been good,
and there had been some well-founded fears for
her physical well-being. But Will said, "We
prayed it through together, dear brother, and we
have seen a miracle."

It was a clear, sunny day three months later.
Margaret and Will, Mrs. Robson (Margaret's
mother), Wallace, Marion, and myself were together by an improvised pulpit under the tall
tabi trees on the main lawn of the mission station. I had been asked to dedicate John to God in
this lovely, tranquil setting. Here the native people could crowd around and watch and feel they
were having a part in what was going on. At
Wallace's instigation, Ap gave a preliminary and
lengthy explanation of what was about to take
place. Loved friends merged their faith and
prayed for John's early salvation and a life dedicated to the service of the Lord.

These were days of delightful fellowship together. We took part in services in the new bush

church buildings at Warames and Kwibin, as well as at Tsingoropa. A softer attitude in the people was now evident, and we noted how they lingered after church to speak at length with the missionary. In fact some were beginning to pray and give some kind of testimony, but Will, as yet, saw no evidence of any spiritual reality among them.

The time came for us to leave, for duty was calling with a loud voice from the continent to the south. As we traveled homeward, Will's oft-quoted phrase kept ringing in our minds: "It's coming, dear brother; I **know** it's coming."

* * * * *

It had grieved Will that, year after year, he had not been able to report any souls saved in the Jimi while his brethren from the other stations in the Wahgi could name several won to Christ. The more he prayed, the more burdened he became for the salvation of the people. At the same time, the more he prayed, the greater was his assurance that the longed-for spiritual visitation would come to pass. His hopes and feelings are reflected in an excerpt from his report to his missionary council meeting in August 1966:

"Behold, the Lord's hand is not shortened, that it cannot save; neither his ear heavy, that it cannot hear" (Isaiah 59:1).

These words from the Word of God are very encouraging. In the work among our people they are especially so. We have now been working for a period of six years, and some may think that in this time we should see greater things than we do for our labors. It seems to me that the essential thing in the early years of primitive work is to lay a solid foundation on which to build. This is what we are seeking to do.

There must be the time of sowing before the harvest. The time of reaping the harvest is fast approaching, and I believe that the Holy Spirit is at work in the hearts of our people in every preaching place in the Jimi Valley. We do have to be careful that we do not urge the people to make false decisions, which may be made just to please the missionary. We feel that we should not try to hurry this time of personal decision beyond their spiritual perceptions. What we pray for is a breakthrough and a real work of grace done in their hearts by the Holy Spirit. The time seems almost ripe for such an experience. We earnestly covet real, born-again Christians to form the nucleus of a vital Nazarene church in the Jimi. Is it too much to expect? Not in the light of the above text . . .

In our first two churches we have some who pray and give testimony. The number attending in each preaching place has greatly increased during the latter part of this year. There also seems to be a greater interest and response on the part of each congregation.

During the following six months, increasing numbers of people attended the church services to hear the Word of God. Many of them, though agreeing with its precepts, were either unwilling or unable to apply it to their own hearts. This state of affairs was going on too long, and it troubled Will deeply.

"All Right, Lord, It's Over to You"

BY MARCH OF 1967, Will was reviewing "seven lean years" of missionary endeavor and was ready to fast and pray as never before for the blessing he longed to see and believed God wanted to bestow. Margaret continually encouraged him to hope in God for the fulfillment of his great ambition, so he began "night watches" of agonizing intercession. It was not just a planned program of prayer that he had undertaken but the only kind of exercise in which he could find release for his burdened heart. He had preached and worked and witnessed as faithfully as he knew how, and to all outward indications nothing of any spiritual worth had taken place in the lives of the people. Sleep went from him. Almost all he could do was appeal to God for the salvation of the inhabitants of the Jimi Valley, many by name. He prayed for the congregations at Tsingoropa, Kwibin, and Warames. He pled that deep conviction for sin might settle on the hearts of people—even those he had never met deep in the jungle fastness of the Jimi.

In the predawn darkness of a certain Monday morning, in desperation and brokenness of spirit, Will cried out: "Lord, please show me if, in any way, I am the hindrance to blessing."

God then spoke to his heart in almost audible tones: "Son, you have carried the burden long enough. Why do you not just trust Me to open the windows of heaven?"

He stopped as though to listen closer, but he had heard enough. He cried: "All right, Lord, it's over to You." A sense of ineffable wonder filled Will's heart; a soul-pervading peace had come and an undeniable assurance that God had now taken over and was already at work. Never before had he experienced such a release in his spirit, nor had he been so aware of being merely an instrument in God's hands rather than a worker **for** God and the mission. Physically depleted from long seasons of prayer, he slept peacefully to awaken a few hours later that morning, jubilant and with that wonderful spirit of expectancy that often comes before blessing.

Will went to church the following Sunday eager and joyful. While delivering his message, he sensed the sweet influences of the Divine Presence. However, at the close there was no visible response from any of the people. The same consciousness of the nearness of God characterized the services on the next four or five Sundays, still with no outward evidences of any of the people turning to God. However, one incident reported later by Will held one faint gleam of hope that the message was getting through:

> One of the tribal leaders came to me after the service and said: "Out there at Kudjip they have many Christians. You have been here for seven years and still we have no Christians. There must be something wrong." I said, "Yes, there is. Do you think I am to blame?" The chief replied, "No." "Then," I said, "it must be you." To this he made no reply but turned and left immediately.

It was not long afterward that Alu made his peace with God and became a true Christian. This had such a remarkable effect on other members of his tribe that almost a score of them turned to the Lord the following Sunday.

An awful awareness of guilt before God and a frightening conviction that their sins would damn their souls gripped the hearts of many. The arrows of the Almighty were finding their marks. Almost every Sunday a few souls were seeking the Lord and finding mercy. Others, already rejoicing in God's grace, were excitedly waiting their turn for the opportunity to testify to the reality of their newfound faith.

In this flood tide of revival blessing, Ap wept his way back to the spiritual experience he once knew while Will shared his tears and prayed at his side. Oura, his wife, found the Lord, too, as well as Mininga and Talya (TAHL-ee-ah).

The fire was not only burning at Tsingoropa but also spreading to Kwibin and Warames. Will told the story of just a few people with whom he had not had any previous acquaintance. They had experienced no contact with the mission and, as far as he could tell, had neither heard of God nor knew anything of the gospel story. These people were stricken with conviction for their sins in the solitude of the jungle and prayed to One they had only then and there become aware of. Peace came to their hearts. Soon afterward they found their way to the mission at Tsingoropa to testify and have their faith confirmed as they learned the way of the Lord more perfectly.

Such a one was Tsiki (SEE-kee), who lived at mountaintop Kwibin. His wife had just been converted and on returning home told him the thrilling news of her salvation through Christ. Tsiki had no understanding at all of what she was talking about. He had not met Missionary Bromley, had never been to church, and had never heard of God before. Here is part of his story:

> One Saturday, I left home and walked the long way down the mountainside into the bush to try to kill some wild pigs. Afterward, I lay down on the ground and started thinking. While I was sleeping, God came to me in my thoughts. I woke up early the next morning and walked many miles until I came to the church at Tsingoropa, just as God showed me in the night. I gave my tes-

timony then. I heard Mr. Bromley preach and decided to become a Christian. I lost all my past sins. After this, I listened eagerly to every story I could hear from the Bible. When I went back to my house, I told all the people about the love of God and how they could become Christians. I did not want any of them to go to hell when they died.

During the course of the next four or five weeks, Tsiki, with his wife, Mul, taught each member of their tribal line (about 30 people in all) how to pray and find the Savior. Will had good reason to believe that each of them found spiritual reality.

Here is an abridged version of Mul's story:

There was no mission in the Jimi—only a patrol officer at Tabibuga. Then Mr. Bromley came and put up his tent on the land at Tsingoropa. He told about a seed that had life in it, and about God, who made all things, and that He was the only God. He asked us if we knew Him. We did not, and we did not understand what Mr. Bromley meant. He said God was the Father of us all, whether black or white. Then he told us how God had sent Jesus to earth, so He could buy our salvation.

Later, I left off going to church; instead I went into the bush. One day a young girl named Tang became a Christian and came up to Kwibin to teach us how to become Christians. I did not heed her message but began attending church again and kept it up until, one Sunday, Mr. Bromley made a call, and I went forward. I found God and became a Christian then went home and testified to Tsiki. Afterward, when he became a Christian, we started prayer meetings in the bush and taught our people how to be saved. We thank God that many are still Christians today.

Such were the simple testimonies of scores who had been born again. The power of the indwelling Christ was soon evident as men and women, young and old, voluntarily discarded their fetishes, adornments, and face and body paint. Christians were looking like Christians and acting like Christians. Thus the heathen people recognized them and were not slow to question, or even despise, any who, professing their faith in God, did not conduct themselves accordingly. Will had no way of knowing, at that time, exactly how many had been saved, but he guessed there were at least 150 who had come into a real and satisfying experience of grace. Moreover, these days of blessedness were continuing as the Holy Spirit sought and saved an expanding group of awakened men and women.

It was early November 1967, only seven months since the first stirrings of the awakening, when Will and Margaret had to face the jarring fact that they were about to leave these people for a time. Their furlough was due. They were to visit Australia, Europe, and the United States and attend the General Assembly in Kansas City in June of the following year. There was no shrinking from what they felt to be their obligation to the program of the church, but it pained them deeply to leave the new Christians at that time. However, their work was to be left in the safe hands of Wallace and Mona White during their one year of absence, and this gave them no small measure of comfort.

The Sunday before their departure, Will faced a sorrowful congregation as he preached his final message. Halfway through, his loved interpreter, Ap, was unable to continue. He sat down with his head in his hands and sobbed, grief-stricken at the thought of soon having to say good-bye to his esteemed *Masta* Bromley. Will had to find another interpreter in order to conclude his message.

The day they left Tabibuga many came from the station to the airstrip to say good-bye. As the plane taxied out for takeoff, they saw small groups of people here and there crying and in deep distress.

The Homegoing

THE YEAR ON FURLOUGH seemed long and travel-packed. General Assembly was a blessing, and the opportunity to meet other missionaries at the great missionary convention in Kansas City was heartwarming and enriching. Wallace had not failed to keep Will and Margaret informed concerning the progress of their work in the Jimi, but Will was becoming restive and eager to get back to Tsingoropa.

They returned to Australia in August 1968 to complete what was needed in their deputation work and to spend two or three weeks with Brother Clem and his wife in Brisbane. During this period, Will was not feeling well, which occasioned a serious conflict of opinion between him and Margaret (their only one). She was determined he should see a doctor; he was determined he should not. They left Townsville, Queensland, by air for Port Moresby on the first of October, soon to be home on their field of labor. They received a joyful and heartmoving welcome by the native Christians.

Under Wallace's care, the work of God had continued to prosper. With his usual aggressive planning, he had three new church buildings erected at Tsingoropa, Kwibin, and Warames to replace the old bush ones that had well served their purpose.

Ap was blossoming in his pastoral work and accepting more and more responsibility. He was now able to tell that God had really called him to be a minister of the gospel right after he was converted as a boy in the Wahgi valley, 10 years before. Churches were now being organized. Ap was to be pastor at Tsingoropa; Mininga, at Kwibin; and Kaowi and Napil had come in from the Wahgi, under Wallace's direction, to assume pastoral care of the Warames and Tabibuga churches, respectively.

In January 1969 the first class of candidates had qualified for baptism. Wallace came in to Tsingoropa to officiate on this important occasion, as Will was not feeling well enough to cope with the physical effort involved in immersing the long line of believers. On the lower terrace, at the foot of a cliff, a baptismal pool had been constructed, which was fed by a clear, perennial spring from the mountainside. There Will stood with the great crowd that had gathered. Tears of joy flowed as these redeemed children of God— his new brothers and sisters—confessed their faith in the living Christ.

This spiritual awakening in the Jimi was not just a great avalanche of blessing to subside within a few months but rather a continuing and steady stream of righteousness. Seekers kept on coming, week by week, to find release for their sin-burdened hearts. God's Holy Spirit was continuing His work.

Will's health, however, was showing no sign of improvement. He was able to work only part of each day, resting often to recoup his strength. He would go to bed for a day or two only to get up again and work when he felt equal to the demands. Will thought he had a prolonged attack of the flu.

To add to Will's discomfort, he slipped and broke his leg just above the ankle. He was flown out to the hospital at Kudjip to have the leg placed in a cast. A week later he returned to the Jimi to pursue his program as best he could within his physical limitations. The cast was removed early in February, and also about this time he began to feel a little better in his general health. The situation was encouraging.

It was learned that Dr. and Mrs. Coulter planned to arrive at Tsingoropa on February 26 to spend a couple of days with them. Will was overjoyed at the prospect of being able to show the general superintendent and his wife living evidences of the power of gospel in the Jimi Valley and have them meet many radiant native Christians. It was also planned for Dr. Coulter to dedicate the new church buildings at Tsingoropa, Kwibin, and Warames.

Accompanied by Wallace, the distinguished

visitors duly arrived, and Margaret and Will were quick to sense their love and concern for them and their work. During their first evening meal together, however, Will took ill again and was forced to leave the table and lie down for the remainder of the evening.

The native people around Tsingoropa, heathen as well as Christian, were now distressfully aware that *Masta* Bromley's health was failing. The following day a group of them, which included Alu and Koroma, sought an audience with Dr. Coulter and expressed their feelings to him with heartmoving words:

> For many years we lived in New Guinea as a primitive people. We had no schools, no church, no hope. But the Nazarenes sent a missionary. He loved us. He told us of Jesus, who loved us. Now there are Christians! *Masta* Bromley has worn himself out for us. Most of us cannot read or write. We want to learn. We want to read God's Word. Will you please send us a missionary to help Missionary Bromley?

Owing to Will's continued illness and the prevailing unsettled weather, the dedication services had to be postponed indefinitely. Will and Margaret bade farewell to Dr. and Mrs. Coulter, grateful to God for their help and guidance and the inspiration of their visit.

Will had been having periodic spasms of pain in the chest, arms, and back and complained of a "dry throat," but he still blamed the flu and fought off any suggestion to go to Kudjip for hospitalization. However, he reluctantly promised Margaret and Wallace that, if he made no progress within the next week or so, he would go to the hospital. Meanwhile, he continued to perform light duties around the station.

On Saturday, March 15, Will experienced severe chest pain that Margaret thought to be a heart attack. That did it. He was taken immediately to Tabibuga, but because of dense cloud cover in the late evening, no plane was able to come in. The patrol officer, Bob Kelvin, and his wife courteously gave Will, Margaret, and John hospitality for the night. Early the next morning, Sunday, they were picked up and flown to the new airstrip at Kudjip. Will was immediately transferred to the hospital, where he received the loving care of Dr. Glen Irwin, Dr. Evelyn Ramsey, and the dedicated staff.

Meanwhile, Wallace and Mona, who were visiting Madang on the north coast of the island, heard the news but were prevented from returning immediately by inclement weather. They finally arrived at the station about 2:15 P.M. on Wednesday, March 19, and Wallace went immediately to Will's bedside. Not wanting to strain the patient, Wallace talked with his colleague for about two minutes, then had prayer with him and left, promising to return within a few hours.

About 4 P.M., with Margaret at his bedside, Will was sitting up enjoying a cup of tea that she had just prepared for him. He had turned toward her as if to speak when he had a sudden seizure and fell forward. She laid him gently back on the bed. There was another spasm, and he slipped away to be with Christ.

Dr. Irwin was at Margaret's side immediately and proved to be a tower of strength and unfailing comfort to her. Wallace was called at once. Shocked and grief-stricken, he was joined by the other missionaries, who offered their loving sympathy to the bereaved. The news was radioed to the Jimi, where Ap became prostrate with grief and where crying broke out all over the valley and continued late into the night.

10

Love's Legacy

PREPARATIONS WERE MADE for the funeral services. The kind hands of David Maloona and Aristaka Narara, two outstanding native Christian young men stationed at Kudjip, fashioned a casket as a final gift of love to the Jimi Valley pioneer.

The following morning at ten o'clock, the funeral service was conducted in the Sidney Knox Memorial Church at Kudjip. All the missionaries had gathered to mourn their loss and rejoice in heaven's gain. Bruce Blowers gave the following eulogy, which echoed the heartfelt sentiments of the missionaries who had known Will and worked with him:

William Bromley was one of us. His passing has left a gap in our ranks. Will walked into our lives in late 1955. Both he and our family were laboring in another mission at that time, and Will walked 35 miles to visit us. Through our short acquaintance with him at that time, we learned a little bit about Will and his past. We realized

76

that he was a man that had tasted sorrow, a man that had experienced God, a man whose ministry had been blessed of God in former years in Australia; and we also learned that he was a man who was committed to serve God and to serve these people in New Guinea.

William Bromley was a pioneer missionary in a sense that none of us has ever been. He came to Kudjip, and then he pioneered the advance into the Tun area, and from there he pioneered the advance into the Tsingoropa area in the Jimi Valley; and he also did some pioneering into the Arami.

Through the years of service, there are a few characteristics about Will that I have noticed and that have stood out to me. First, was his willingness to witness for Christ. I don't believe that Will knew black or white, but all men were God's children. He ministered in a spiritual way to those whom he met. And Will established close friendships. Long before he was married and had a son, he had sons and daughters among these people, people that he had loved and had borne upon his heart before God until they were brought into the saving knowledge of Christ.

Because Will has been with us, the love of Christ has been shed abroad in a deeper way in our own lives. Our lives have been made richer. Heaven holds more hope and each of us has been challenged by the example of a missionary with soul concern, with compassion for others—the kind of concern that each of us should have. And because of this, I believe that the work of William Bromley's life will live on in the years to come.

After the service, the casket was moved to the nearby airstrip for the flight to Tabibuga to fulfil Will's long-ago-stated request: "When I die, I want to be buried in the Jimi." Wallace traveled beside the casket on this lone and sad journey. Bob Kelvin had a government vehicle ready at the airstrip to take Wallace, with the casket, over the familiar trail in Tsingoropa. This accomplished, the vehicle was driven back to the airstrip to pick up the small group of mourners who had arrived on a second plane. These were Margaret, Mona White, Wanda Knox, Dr. Irwin, Daryl Schendel, and the government officer and his wife.

A great crowd of natives had gathered at the graveside on the lower terrace not far from Will's prized "orchidarium." They had been crying most of the day, but when the missionaries arrived, they gave full expression to their pent-up grief. Wallace was in charge of the simple committal service.

The party from Kudjip, except Wallace, had to make their way back quickly to Tabibuga for the flight home, as night would soon be upon them. Immediately after their departure, the people again gave vent to unrestrained crying and wailing. After about 20 minutes of such audible distress, Ap began to silence the people. He then broke down himself; but after regaining his composure, he recounted the story from the time he was a school boy when Brother Bromley first went with him to the Tun area and stayed with his tribe there. He said that *Masta* Bromley was the same as a father, and he had no other father like the missionary. He told about some of the experiences he and Brother Bromley had had together, how they came into the Jimi Valley and how he had been taught by him. Now *Masta* Bromley was dead.

Then he said: "Oh, everything inside me pains," upon which the floodgates of grief broke open once more. He bowed himself over the casket and, in the Kuma language, cried: "Danjip! Danjip!" ("Father! Father!") Then he used the more intimate term: "Dapo! Dapo!" ("Dear Father! Dear Father!") Where are you?" This he did at least a score of times; and when it was almost dark and Wallace could wait no longer, Ap gave his consent for the casket to be lowered.

With the heart of a true shepherd, Wallace remained with Ap and Oura overnight and late into the next day. According to native custom, they talked at length about the days that were important to them in their relationships with Missionary Bromley. Wallace arranged for Ap to look after the Tsingoropa station, assist the other pastors with their several needs, and take charge of the daily radio contact with Kudjip.

Margaret remained at Kudjip for 10 days. Although Wallace and Mona pressed her to stay longer and rest, the pull of the Jimi was too strong, so she and John went back to Tsingoropa to try to dry their tears and bravely face the demands of the tomorrows.

* * * * *

It was July 22, 1969, when I again accompanied Wallace into Tabibuga. Margaret and Little John were at the airstrip to greet us. It became difficult to adjust to Will's absence while moving around the Jimi. He had come and gone, but the godly influence of his life had left its mark upon many. I recognized several people whom I had previously known and who were now wearing the "light of life" on their faces.

The light of the gospel still shone in the darkness of the Jimi, but many in that darkness were still resisting its revealing power. There were not a few who knew what they ought to do to find God but would not pay the price. Such was one of the chiefs who had been subject to some degree of spiritual awakening after several members of his tribe had found Christ.

This man sat with Wallace, Mininga, and others around the fire one night, talking about certain Christian standards that were apparently troubling him. He wanted *God's tok* for sure, but he wanted some of the old ways as well. Wallace was, of course, firm in maintaining Bible emphases while giving the answer to the chief's problem. He pointed out that God's ways are best for all of us. The chief replied: "What you have said hits us like an arrow hits a bird and breaks its wing. We cannot fly with one wing." He left that conference unwilling to yield to God and unable to understand that "they that wait upon the Lord . . . shall mount up with wings as eagles" (Isaiah 40:31).

It was thrilling to learn that 126 Christians had already been baptized. Forty-nine adults and 35 young people were attending classes, with others already having found God and many more beginning to comprehend the way of life for the first time.

It was beautiful to see Ap and Oura united in the Lord. Margaret described Oura as "a gem." Ap and I talked happily together recounting old times, but when sympathy was expressed to him concerning his loss in the passing of Brother Bromley, he at once turned, bowed his head, and walked quickly away.

On Wednesday, July 23, there occurred an event unique in the history of the Jimi Valley. It was a peace ceremony between two tribes that had been enemies from ancient times but had now been touched by the love of God. They had one last "mock battle" and then ate together, symbolizing a new, lasting peace between them and giving the people of the Jimi Valley a strong testimony to the transforming power of the gospel. To this, we added the witness of the dedication of the three new church buildings at

Warames, Tsingoropa, and Kwibin over the next three days.

During the dedication services, with Wallace giving guidance, we talked about symbols: the cross, the spire, the altar, and other things related to the church. Their meanings and significance were explained. (The native culture is rich in symbolism, so with this approach the people would be more likely to understand.) These brief discourses, which were gospel-blended, were followed by the dedications. Afterward the second chapter of Acts from the New Testament in pidgin *(Nupela Testamen)* was read and interpreted. Ap then gave his talk on the fire of Pentecost with calm composure and an easy command. When he spoke, all was quiet and attention was undivided. It was clear that he had the respect of the people and that the anointing of God was upon him.

Beginning at Warames on Thursday, Napil, the pastor at Tabibuga, brought a small, lighted kerosene lamp into the church and with it lit a small metal bowl containing wood alcohol, which had been placed there by Kaowi, the Warames pastor. Tongues of fire leaped upward. At the close, Ap lit his lamp from this fire and took it to Tsingoropa, where the process was repeated the following day. Mininga then took the fire to Kwibin for the third day, where it burned again on the altar.

Ap explained the symbolism of the act in this way:

The Holy Spirit came down in tongues of fire at Pentecost, and that fire is still burning. It is our duty to keep it burning. *Masta* Bromley came into the Jimi Valley and brought the fire. Now that *Masta* Bromley has gone to heaven, Mininga, Kaowi, Napil, Ap, and other Christians must carry the flame so it will spread from Christian to heathen until we are all burning for God.

After bidding farewell to the Christians, I pondered: Why was God able to use William Bromley so remarkably? Was he specially favored? No! That could not be. God does not have any favorites. But He does have His intimates, and Will chose to be one of them. He lived close to God, just like William Carey, who went to India as a missionary in 1793 and also labored for seven years before he baptized his first convert.

* * * * *

Will's bees have now gone wild and multiplied to produce their sweetness in tree trunk, rock cleft, and mountain gorge. His flowers still grace the mountains and valleys in increasing numbers to charm those who tread the highland trails. The sweetness and fragrance of his Christ-centered life still linger to inspire others to walk with God, just as he did.

▸▸▸ EPILOGUE

"The Rest of the Story"
BY ROBERT H. SCOTT

"THE REST OF THE STORY"—It's a phrase made famous by Paul Harvey, one of North America's best known newscasters. In his gifted communication style, he introduces his listeners to intriguing personal interest stories, and then carries them out to surprising.

This is "the rest of the story" begun on the previous pages of this book in the words written by Dr. A. A. E. Berg. More than 25 years have now passed since William Ewart Bromley was laid to rest in an isolated grave in Papua New Guinea's Jimi Valley. In the 19 previous years, his life was a remarkable living sacrifice of love for his beloved adopted people.

When death silenced his voice and stilled his hands, there was yet much unfulfilled in the dreams of this tireless pioneer missionary. With the culture being so primitive and the work location being so isolated, one would understandably wonder if the scattered seeds could hold their tender root systems and survive beyond the sorrowful and unexpected encounter with death.

To make matters worse, this was not the first time death had cut short a key life with noble intention for Nazarene missions in the colorful land surrounded by Coral seas. Twelve years earlier, Sidney and Wanda Knox, who first opened Nazarene ministry in Papua New Guinea, were compelled to make an unexpected and unwanted departure from the country when malignancy gripped Sidney's body. A short three years of labor came to sudden end, and brief months later Sidney was laid to rest, his hands also having been stilled by the unwanted intruder called death.

With two such dynamic pioneer missionaries removed prematurely from that land, what would be the effect on the long-range development of the new church? Time alone could tell.

Time now has told, and that is the intriguing "rest of the story."

* * * * *

It was a humid January morning in 1994. A short while before, I had climbed aboard a Missionary Aviation Fellowship twin-engine airplane. The itinerary of that day included a stop in isolated Sangaape, location of a Nazarene medical clinic, and Dusan, center of some of our most isolated evangelistic work in Papua New Guinea. On the way back to Mount Hagen airport, we hoped to drop in at the famous Jimi Valley.

By the time the other two stops were made, a huge cumulus cloud buildup over the jungle mountains was turning ugly. At first we thought we would not even be able to see the Jimi Valley, and a landing in the mounting negative weather condition was ruled out. Just before heading west back toward Mount Hagen, however, there was an unexpected break in the cloud system and before us in all its colorful uniqueness lay "the Jimi." With no intention to land, the pilot brought the plane in low, and pointed out the building with the largest roof exposure. "That," he said, "is your Jimi Valley Nazarene church."

I had reason to feel a special sense of pride. In the early 1980s when my wife, Carolyn, was district NWMS president on the Southern California District, she had presented a Papua New Guinea project, and faithful Nazarenes had quickly given more than $20,000. Months later, a Work and Witness team had come to this place and erected an impressive building. It was another chapter in the ongoing saga of the Jimi Valley story begun years before by Will Bromley.

Looking out the window of the airplane, I knew that a short distance from that church building was the grave holding the earthly remains of Will Bromley. It was disappointing to be so close and not be able to actually touch the soil. There was, however, special satisfaction in the "view from above." I was aware that by now "the rest of the story" was a clearly established positive fact.

The progress of the church had not been buried or even impaired when Will Bromley went to heaven, leaving those grieving mourners to feel his loss. Indeed, as evidenced by the commodious facility that lay beneath us, the work he started grew steadily larger in numbers and influence. The arrows of the Almighty continued to find their mark in thousands of Papua New Guinea lives.

* * * * *

Many things remain the same today as they were when Will Bromley arrived alone in 1950 to begin his work of love, and when Sidney and Wanda Knox commenced Nazarene work here in 1955. The clock that most of the world calls "progress" moves slowly in the land called Papua New Guinea.

It remains one of the world's most primitive cultures. The tropical jungles have had amazingly little invasion by modern explorers or tourists. The people (population now numbers 4.5 million) continue living much as their ancestors lived for generations and centuries of time.

Papua New Guinea is a society structured around a thousand distinct tribes, most of which speak their own language dialect. This little nation, therefore, has the distinction of speaking more languages than any other nation on earth. Given its linguistic and cultural uniqueness, it is considered to be one of the world's most ethnically complex places.

War has always been a way of life between the tribes. Conflicts are regularly triggered over such issues as land boundaries or over such other seemingly incongruous issues as a misplaced pig! The weapons of warfare remain essentially (and fortunately!) primitive: bows, arrows, axes—though a new trend is now emerging with guns (many homemade) being increasingly used as instruments for conflict.

The country of Papua New Guinea has no elaborate road systems to facilitate transportation and communication or to help bring its people together in a sense of common society. Only one main highway artery exists, stretching from the coastal city of Lae up into the highlands. Besides this, there are scattered mountain and flatland roads crudely built by local communities, often with the simplest of equipment but inadequate for most travel by vehicle. For some of the remote settlements, the government has constructed airstrips, giving isolated tribes their only link with the outside world apart from the long, winding walking trails.

Roughly 70 percent of the people of the country still live by primitive standards, relying on subsistence gardening and farming. The practice of hunting and fishing is common as the people engage in their domestic survival practices.

Some economic impact is beginning to be realized by recent years' discoveries of rich mineral deposits and natural gas resources. These discoveries will increasingly force changes, and, with sudden wealth falling into unready hands, not all of the changes will result in good for the people.

Education is still a luxury for most of the people. Barely 43 percent of the population is literate. Religious freedom is one of the country's assets, and intense missionary activity by many different religious groups in recent years is helping push back the darkness of superstition and animism. Most people are now identified in nominal "Christian" categories. It is significant that the Church of the Nazarene, during its relatively short history in the country, has become one of the most influential religious movements in the nation.

Since the initial exploratory trip made by Dr. Berg in 1954 and the arrival of our first missionaries, Sidney and Wanda Knox, in 1955, the Church of the Nazarene has grown to a membership of over 7,000. When Will Bromley died there were four churches in the Jimi Valley, and only 11 Nazarene churches in the country. There are now 24 churches in the Jimi Valley, and some 300 churches and preaching points in the country (159 organized churches were reported in 1994). These churches are divided into seven organized districts with six of these being led by national district superintendents.

Though the work of early leaders Sidney Knox and Will Bromley was tragically and prematurely cut off by their deaths, Jesus has continued to build His Church. "The rest of the story" is one of our most thrilling records of missionary effectiveness and national church development.

* * * * *

Evangelism continues to be the primary purpose and thrust of the Nazarene mission program in Papua New Guinea. This has been greatly aided by strong long-term career missionaries like Mona and Wallace White, Ruth and Bruce Blowers, Joyce and Neville Bartle, Myrna and Bob Dipert, Pat and Gordon Johnston, and others!

Natalie and Vern Ward, starting out as specialized lay workers on a temporary mission to Papua New Guinea, became captivated by the people and gave themselves to this country. They and their four young children went to live in Dusan, one of the most isolated outstations in the entire Church of the Nazarene.

The only access the Wards had to Dusan was by Missionary Aviation Fellowship airplane. No other expatriates lived in the area. Shopping for groceries had to be accomplished via radio from Mount Hagen, and delivery was by the monthly arrival of the small aircraft. They walked the rugged trails and astonished the people of the area by showing them their first white faces. When the Wards moved to a new assignment in early 1994, there were Nazarene churches all across the canyons and hills. It was a classic example of the noble spirit of evangelism that drove Will Bromley and has continued to drive

Nazarene missionaries through our brief history in the country.

* * * * *

The passion to provide education has walked hand in hand with evangelism in the Nazarene mission work in Papua New Guinea. The Nazarene system is always, everywhere, to train national Christians so that they are equipped to understand better the way of the gospel and enabled to communicate it to their own countrymen.

Early in the Nazarene Papua New Guinea story, missionaries Carol and Lee Eby established a Nazarene Bible College along the road between Mount Hagen and Kudjip. This stunningly beautiful setting, surrounded by ever-green hills and neatly trimmed tea plantations, now is developed into an excellent campus for both classroom training and student housing.

A long and illustrious list of Nazarene missionary educators graced this campus in the past and give it strength and purpose today. Following the retirement of long-term career missionaries Helen and Ray Bolerjack, Linda and Gary Glassco moved into the principal's home, with Gary assuming that office. More than 100 young men and women are now enrolled, and each year a fine class of graduates goes out to further strengthen the indigenous church of Papua New Guinea. In the distant capital city of Port Moresby, an English level advanced education program is now being offered.

Tomorrow's church leaders will be well equipped as "the rest of the story" continues to be supplemented and written out through the work of Nazarene missionary educators and their dedicated students.

* * * * *

When the Nazarene mission program commenced in 1955, the primitive and undeveloped nature of the country of Papua New Guinea was dramatically demonstrated by the absence of adequate health care and conditions for the people. It was natural, therefore, that early concerns included the desire and vision to bring the healing arts to Papua New Guinea's people as a ministry of the church.

Beginning with a vision embraced by both Dr. Berg and General Superintendent Hardy C. Powers, it first expressed itself with Wanda Knox's "backdoor dispensary." Missionary nurse Margaret Robson, who later became Margaret Bromley, was a vital part of that evolving medical program from the time she came to the country until her retirement in 1993. She worked in the Jimi Valley, at the hospital in Kudjip, and finally in remote Sangaape.

The 100-bed hospital was officially opened March 31, 1967, and dedicated by Dr. Powers. Following a year of initial struggle, the arrival of Dr. and Mrs. Glen Irwin in 1968 commenced a record of expanding medical efficiency and notoriety across the highlands of Papua New

Guinea, and, indeed, throughout the entire country. Today a large staff of medical missionaries—doctors, nurses, and other professional support staff—are joined by national personnel being trained in Nazarene Nursing College to operate what is called the nation's best medical facility.

Community health extension programs and village health evangelism efforts have always taken the work of the hospital far beyond its boundaries in Kudjip. In Sangaape, accessible only by Missionary Aviation Fellowship airplane, the remote Nazarene clinic begun by Margaret Bromley after Will's death is now staffed by Janet and Warren Neal, Nazarene medical missionaries.

Here the physically beautiful setting of hill and jungle holds a compound including the missionary home, a church, and the medical clinic buildings. Here people regularly come after walking long distances over long trails, bringing such physical problems as broken bones, wounds and infections, birth complications, dysentery, numerous children's diseases, and malnourishment.

Assisted by their Kudjip-trained national nurse team, the missionaries there minister to both bodies and souls. People of the Sangaape area live and look like the people who have been there for centuries, totally removed from so-called modernization. They are, however, slowly being brought into a better physical way of life, and more importantly into a better spiritual way of life.

The thousands of Papua New Guinea people who are benefactors every year of Nazarene medical missions are part of "the rest of the story" that began in the adventurous heart of such pioneers as A. A. E. Berg, Sidney and Wanda Knox, and Will Bromley. In a January 1994 meeting with Mr. Pius Wingti, prime minister of Papua New Guinea, I listened as he expressed his appreciation for the church's medical work with his people. "There is no finer organization for health services in my country," he declared, "than that given by the Church of the Nazarene."

* * * * *

So, the arrows of the Almighty continue to strike, carrying out the early vision and dream of pioneer Will Bromley. Many of the instruments of spiritual progress are the converts introduced in earlier pages of this book.

Faithful Ap continued to pastor in the Jimi after Will Bromley's death and was one of the first group of pastors to be ordained in Papua New Guinea in 1977. Eventually he left the Jimi and returned to his home area of Tun where he continues to pastor the Tun Nazarene church.

Many young people from the Jimi Valley churches have attended Nazarene Bible College. Most of these graduated and returned to pastor new churches that had sprung up in the Jimi area. Others have gone to be pioneer church planters in even more remote parts of the Middle Ramu District.

* * * * *

"The rest of the story" continues to be told and written. Papua New Guinea Nazarenes have now taken initiative for the beginning of the work of the Church of the Nazarene in Solomon Islands, a chain of islands several hundred miles east of their country.

Wallace and Mona White moved to Guadalcanal, the most famous of the Solomons, to help initiate this work as their final assignment before retirement. Assisting them in its commencement, and remaining to carry on the work after their departure, are Rev. and Mrs. Andrew Moime, Nazarene elder and wife from Papua New Guinea. Nazarenes in that country have no intention to be simply receivers of the good news brought through historic missionary efforts. Having received, they now join the ranks of givers and senders and have begun to share the gospel with the spiritually unenlightened in lands far away from them.

Postscript

In the "Dedication" paragraph of the original edition of the book *Arrows of the Almighty*, it is interesting to read Dr. A. A. E. Berg's lines expressing the hope that "the selflessness and Christian fragrance which characterized the life

of Missionary William Ewart Bromley be reflected in his young son, John William, to whom this
book is affectionately dedicated."

Through the grace of God and the influence
of a godly father and mother, that "dedication"
has become a fulfilled "prophecy." John William
Bromley, now a grown man in his early adult
years, has given himself to a continuing ministry
in the tradition of his wonderful father and
mother. John has taken assignment with Missionary Aviation Fellowship, intending to serve as a
pilot in Papua New Guinea! The organization
that first carried his father to the isolated Jimi
Valley will have John's skilled hands and dedicated heart, continuing to serve such isolated
peoples and places as his father served a quarter
century ago. How fitting! It is inconceivable to
imagine a better "rest of the story" than this!